# Investigating our local area

## and the wider world

Caroline Clissold

**www.heinemann.co.uk/library**

Visit our website to find out more information about **Heinemann Library** books.

To order:
☎ Phone 44 (0) 1865 888066
📄 Send a fax to 44 (0) 1865 314091
💻 Visit the Heinemann Bookshop at www.heinemann.co.uk/library to browse our catalogue and order online.

First published in Great Britain by Heinemann Library, Halley Court, Jordan Hill, Oxford OX2 8EJ, part of Harcourt Education. Heinemann is a registered trademark of Harcourt Education Ltd.

© Harcourt Education Ltd 2006
The moral right of the proprietor has been asserted.

Editorial: Vicki Yates
Design: Dave Poole and Tokay Interactive Limited (www.tokay.co.uk)
Illustrations: Geoff Ward and International Mapping (www.internationalmapping.com)
Picture Research: Hannah Taylor
Production: Duncan Gilbert

Originated by Repro Multi Warna
Printed in China by WKT Company Limited

10 digit ISBN: 0 431 03251 3    (Hardback)
13 digit ISBN: 978 0 431 03251 1 (Hardback)
10 09 08 07 06
10 9 8 7 6 5 4 3 2 1

10 digit ISBN: 0 431 03258 0    (Paperback)
13 digit ISBN: 978 0 431 03258 0 (Paperback)
10 09 08 07 06
10 9 8 7 6 5 4 3 2 1

**British Library Cataloguing in Publication Data**
Clissold, Caroline
Investigating the local area and the wider world
910
A full catalogue record for this book is available from the British Library.

**Acknowledgements**
Alamy Images p. **7** (Leslie Garland Picture Library), p. **15** (Duncan Hale-Sutton), p. **22** (Justin Kase); Conwy County Borough Council pp. **10**, **11**; Corbis p. **4** (Stocktrek), p. **19b** (Kristi J. Black), p. **24** (Stephen Frink), p. **27** (Yann Arthus-Bertrand); Edinburgh & Lothians Networks office p. **8**; Photodisc p. **12**; Photolibrary.com p. **25**; PRM Marketing Ltd p. **9**; Reproduced by permission of Ordnance Survey on behalf of The Controller of Her Majesty's Stationery Office, © Crown Copyright 100000230 pp. **6**, **20**; Rex features p. **23** (Marius Alexander); Skyscan p. **21** (B Evans); TopFoto pp. **17**, **19t** (Woodmansterne); Topham Picturepoint p. **29**.

Cover photograph of a satellite image of the Earth, reproduced with permission of Corbis/Stocktrek.

The publishers would like to thank Rebecca Harman, Rachel Bowles, Robyn Hardyman, and Caroline Landon for their assistance in the preparation of this book.

Every effort has been made to contact copyright holders of any material reproduced in this book. Any omissions will be rectified in subsequent printings if notice is given to the publishers.

All the Internet addresses (URLs) given in this book were valid at the time of going to press. However, due to the dynamic nature of the Internet, some addresses may have changed, or sites may have changed or ceased to exist since publication. While the author and Publishers regret any inconvenience this may cause readers, no responsibility for any such changes can be accepted by either the author or the Publishers.

## Exploring further

Throughout this book you will find links to the Heinemann Explore CD-ROM and website at www.heinemannexplore.com. Follow the links to find out more about the topic.

# Contents

Any words appearing in the text in bold, **like this**, are explained in the glossary.

# Where is our local area in relation to other places?

By studying geography we can learn a lot about different places around the world, including the place where we live. One way to do this is to look at maps and photographs. Your local library will have maps – both old and new – showing continents, countries, cities, towns, and villages. You could also look at a wide variety of photographs, including **aerial photographs** and **satellite photographs**.

■ *This picture of Earth was taken from a satellite in space.*

### Looking for the UK

Do you know how to find the United Kingdom (UK) on a map of the world? Think about which part of the world the UK is in. You may know that the UK is part of Europe and that it is an island. This should help you to find it.

### Getting closer

Think about your location within the UK. Are you in the north, south, east, or west? Are you by the **coast** or inland? These things should help you to find where you live on a map.

■ *You can look on a map of the UK to work out where your village, town, or city is.*

## Where is our school?

When you have worked out where you live on a map of the UK, you can look at large-scale maps, such as Ordnance Survey (OS) maps or street maps. With these detailed maps you can find out lots of information, such as where your school is, or where there is a post office or a church. You can also find these places on maps on some websites on the Internet by typing in your postcode or a place name. These maps sometimes also have matching aerial or satellite photographs.

## Look around

Maps and photographs also tell us about what a **locality** is like. If you look at an aerial photograph of the area around your school, what features do you see? Make a list of what you can see on this aerial photograph.

# What do we expect places to be like?

## Getting the information

To discover what a place is like, you can use a variety of **secondary sources** of information. This means that you are given the information from somewhere else, not from actually going to the place yourself. You can look for information about places in encyclopaedias and other reference books.

## Maps and pictures

Another important way to learn about a place is to use maps. Maps have information about what the area looks like, which towns and cities are nearby, and where there are rivers and mountains. To get a more accurate idea about a place you can look at pictures of it. You can find these in holiday brochures, tourist leaflets, and in photographs taken by visitors to a place. You can also find information on places using the Internet.

## Activity

You want to find out about the village of Malham in Yorkshire.

1. Use the sources mentioned above to find out everything you can about the village.

2. Make notes and then draw a map of the village as you imagine it.

3. Now look at the map to the right and compare it with your map. Does your map show some of the same things?

4. Look at the photograph of Malham Cove on the opposite page. Can you find this feature on the map? How can you identify it?

■ *This is an Ordnance Survey map of Malham, Yorkshire.*

■ *Malham Cove is a rocky **limestone** crag formed by a waterfall that has now disappeared. It is 80 metres (262 feet) high and 300 metres (984 feet) wide.*

## Answering the question

When you are trying to find out about a place, it is helpful to use headings to organize your research. These are some useful headings:

- location in the UK
- **weather** and water
- goods and services
- leisure and entertainment.

By making notes under each of your headings, you will find you soon have a good idea of what your **locality** might be like.

## Exploring further

On the Heinemann Explore website or CD-ROM go to Exploring > The World. Read the article on Recife in Brazil to find out more about the locality of this city. Look at the photographs and maps that go with the article. What do they tell you about Recife? Think about what it would be like to walk around the city.

# Edinburgh

Let us imagine we will be going on a sightseeing trip to Edinburgh, the **capital city** of Scotland. We want to find out as much as we can about the city before we go there. Using the information on these two pages, work out what you expect Edinburgh to be like.

## Internet

We can use websites on the Internet to find out what there is to do, where we can stay, the history of the city, and what it looks like.

*We can see what there is to do by reading about the attractions.*

*Interesting historical information can give us a feel for past life in the city.*

*Photographs of the city show us what the place will look like.*

*We can use a list of hotels to see where we can stay.*

*Travel information can tell us how to get around the city.*

**Edinburgh.**
The Official Site

Find a Place to Stay.
Special Offers.
What's On.
City & Area Guide.
Practical Information.

Home Page. | City & Area Guide.

### Search Our Listings.

Attractions

Eating and Drinking

Shopping

Entertainment

Sport, Leisure & Activities

Sightseeing & Tours

Accessible Attractions

### More About...

An Historic Capital

Beaches & Coastal Villages

Countryside Walks

Edinburgh Villages

Golf

Royal Edinburgh

Local Crafts and Industries

Historic Houses

Art and Literature

### City & Area Guide.

From 5 star visitor attractions and tours, to fabulous food to suit every taste (and wallet), Edinburgh's got it all.

The city is home to some of the best galleries and museums in the UK, so whether you're into modern art, want to learn more about Scotland's history or fancy a trip down memory lane with the toys of your childhood, the city has something for you.

Add great shopping and world-class theatre to the mix and you really are spoilt for choice. That's where we can help - take a look at the listings below and find your favourite things to do.

### Attractions.

The best attractions - castles, museums and more...

Search Attractions

### Eating & Drinking.

Lots to whet your appetite, whatever your taste.

Search Eating and Drinking

### Shopping.

### Entertainment.

### Find a Place to Stay.

From hotels to hostels, from the city centre to the countryside, wherever you want to stay, find your perfect place.

Search Accommodation

### Edinburgh Convention Bureau.

Conventions don't have to be conventional. Edinburgh's your inspired choice!

More about Edinburgh Convention Bureau

### Getting Here & Getting Around.

**8**

■ *We can discover a lot about a place from a website.*

# Maps

We can use maps to get a feel for the layout of the city, to locate places of interest to us, and to work out the distances between places.

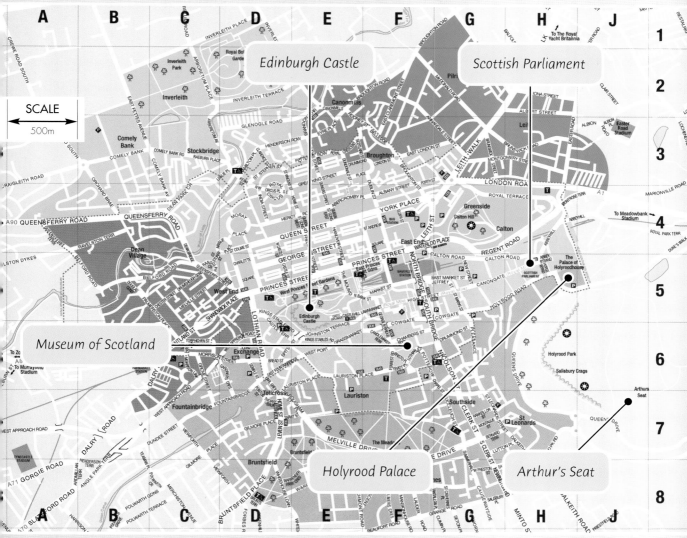

■ This tourist map shows the layout of Edinburgh city centre and the main sights.

## Activity

1 Use the scale on the map above to work out how big Edinburgh is.
2 If you were visiting the city, would you need to take a bus to get from Holyrood Palace to Edinburgh Castle, or could you walk?

9

## Llandudno

Now let us imagine we are going on a weekend break to the town of Llandudno in North Wales. Using all the information on these two pages, work out what you expect Llandudno to be like. Make a list of some things you could do there during your weekend break.

This text describes the landscape.

Here is a brief summary of the main attractions of the town.

The essential pocket guide
### LLANDUDNO
2005

#### SO MUCH TO EXPERIENCE.

TIMELESS ELEGANCE
IN A PERFECT SETTING

Llandudno is one of the finest
traditional seaside resorts in the world.

The setting is perfect. A splendid promenade spans the
gently curving bay between the headlands of the Great
Orme and the Little Orme. And there's a second beach
on the West Shore, with glorious views of Snowdonia
and Anglesey across the Conwy Estuary.

The town is outstandingly preserved, with all the
traditional attractions of its Victorian origins.
And it's a bustling centre for shopping,
entertainment and cultural life, all year round.

#### SO MUCH TO ENJOY.

A WORLD OF ADVENTURE

The Great Orme is a holiday adventure in its own right.

Drive, walk, or take the Victorian tramway or cable car
(Britain's longest) to the top. The views to the Isle of
Man and the Lake District will take your breath away.

Discover 4,000 year old copper mines. Enjoy the birdlife,
flora and fauna. Try the dry ski slope and toboggan run.
Stroll round the Happy Valley gardens. Or take a pot of
tea at the Summit Complex.

Don't forget the Little Orme either, where a short walk
is rewarded with more gorgeous views and a world of
natural wonder.

TRADITION AT ITS BEST

IN ALL SEASONS.
FOR ALL REASONS.

EXOTIC
SHELLS

Photographs of the area show us what Llandudno will look like.

This describes what the view from the top of Great Orme will be like.

■ Tourist leaflets provide information of the main attractions in a place.

It is useful to know where the tourist information centre is. Here you can find out all about what's going on in a place.

The map shows us that the main beach is very long, and that you can walk alongside it on the promenade.

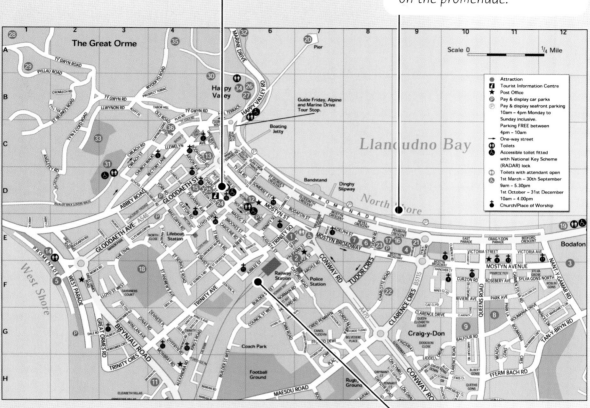

It might help when planning a visit to know that there is a train station in the centre of the town.

## LLANDUDNO

### ATTRACTIONS & PLACES OF INTEREST

| | | |
|---|---|---|
| 1 | Alice in Wonderland Centre | E6 |
| 2 | Oriel Mostyn Art Gallery | E7 |
| 3 | Bodafon Farm Park | F12/13 |
| 4 | Broadway Boulevard | E9 |
| 5 | Children's Play Area | F2 |
| 6 | Citizen's Advice Bureau | E8 |
| 7 | Coach Station | E8 |
| 8 | Craig-y-Don Park | G11 |
| 9 | Craig-y-Don Recreation Ground (bowls and tennis) | G10 |
| 10 | Llandudno Golf Club, Maesdu | I5 |
| 11 | North Wales Golf Club, West Shore | H4 |
| 12 | Library | D6 |
| 13 | Market Hall | C5 |
| 14 | Model Boating Pool | E1 |
| 15 | Amgueddfa Llandudno Museum | D4 |
| 16 | North Wales Conference Centre | E9 |
| 17 | North Wales Theatre | E8 |
| 18 | The Oval Recreation Ground | F3 |
| 19 | Paddling Pool & Play Area | E12 |
| 20 | Pier | A7 |
| 21 | Sailing Club | E9 |
| 22 | Superbowl | F8 |
| 23 | Swimming Pool | E8 |
| 24 | Tourist Information Centre | D5 |
| 25 | World War II – Home Front Experience | D5 |

## THE GREAT ORME

| | | |
|---|---|---|
| 26 | Cable Car | B6 |
| 27 | Camera Obscura | B6 |
| 28 | Great Orme Country Park | A1 |
| 29 | Great Orme Mines | A1 |
| 30 | Happy Valley Gardens | B5 |
| 31 | Haulfre Gardens | D3 |
| 32 | Marine Drive | A5 |
| 33 | Miniature Golf Course | C2 |
| 34 | Putting Green | B5 |
| 35 | Ski Slope & Toboggan Run | A4 |
| 36 | Tram Station | C4 |

Here is a list of the main attractions of the town.

■ This tourist map shows Llandudno and its attractions.

11

# What are places actually like?

## Going on a field trip

In geography, when we want to find out what a place is actually like we need to go there. This is called a **field trip**. On a field trip we study a place for ourselves. This gives us a better idea of what it is like than we can get from **secondary sources**.

### Tasks to do on a field trip

There are two main things that you need to do on a field trip. First, you need to identify the main **physical features** of the area. These are the natural features such as rivers, hills, and woodlands. You should also identify the **human features** of the area. These are all the things made by humans, such as housing, factories, and roads.

The physical features of a place often have an effect on the human features. You will need to think about the layout of the place you are studying, and the ways in which the land is used in different areas.

▪ *Mountains and lakes are physical features of an area.*

## See for yourself

Visit a local village or an area of your town. Think about the layout of the place. Is it all straight roads, or are there short streets and crescents? Do you know why it is laid out in this way? Think about what the different areas of land are used for. Are they used for homes, to create jobs, or for leisure? What might the park be there for? What could people do by the river if there is one? Make notes on your findings.

## Collecting information

There are different ways to collect information about a **locality** on a field trip:

- Draw field sketches showing the main features of the physical landscape and human activity.
- Carry out a land-use survey of the main street and record your findings on a map with a colour-coded **key**.
- Take photographs to help with your labelling of the sketches and maps when you are back at school.

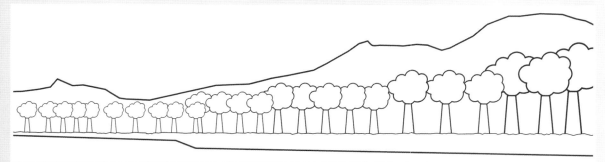

■ *Field sketches are a good way to record information about a locality on a field trip.*

## Back at school

Take your field sketches and land-use maps back to school. Discuss what you have found out, and compare the place you visited with your own local area.

## Exploring further

Find out more about the city of Paris in France on the Heinemann Explore website or CD-ROM. Go to Exploring > Europe and choose the article 'Paris – a city in France'. Look at the photographs that go with it. Think about the layout of the city, and how the different areas of land are used.

# Edinburgh

Edinburgh is the **capital city** of Scotland and the home of Scotland's Parliament. It is in the Central Lowlands of Scotland and is surrounded by the Lothians. To the north is the **coast** of the Firth of Forth, where the River Forth enters the North Sea.

Edinburgh has a number of **ports**, an international airport, and rail links to all the major centres in Britain.

## A popular city

Edinburgh has the second-largest **population** in Scotland after Glasgow. Around 500,000 people live there. With so many people living there, and about two million **tourists** visiting each year, Edinburgh is a busy and lively city.

■ *This map shows the location of Edinburgh.*

Many **tourists** come to visit Edinburgh because it has a rich history. Many buildings survive from the past, which people enjoy visiting. These include the buildings of the Old Town, where people often spend time walking through the cobbled **medieval** streets and alleyways. People also like to visit the many museums and art galleries that the city has to offer.

Perhaps the busiest time of year in Edinburgh is during the festival season. The Edinburgh festival is the biggest arts event in Europe and thousands visit to see plays and exhibitions, to listen to music, and much more. The city is a very exciting place to be at this time.

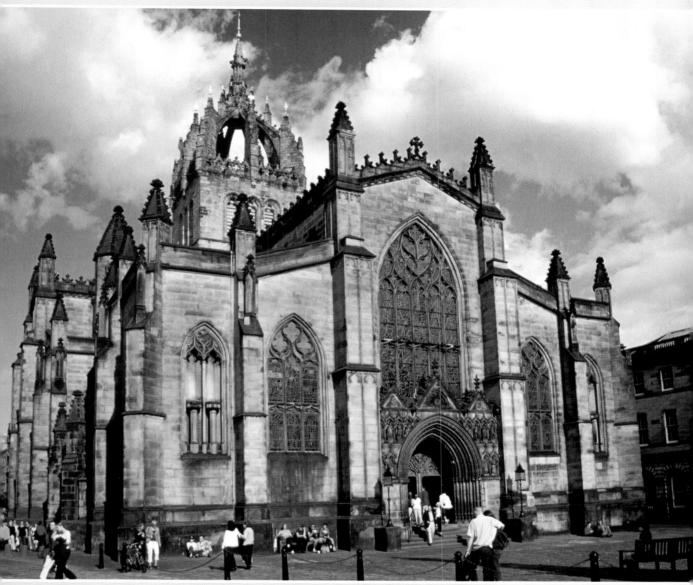

■ *St Giles Cathedral was built in the 1100s and is on the Royal Mile, a famous street in Edinburgh. This is a human feature of the city as it is man-made.*

## Activity

Imagine that you and your friend live in Birmingham and want to visit Edinburgh. You have persuaded a relative to drive you there.

1  Use a road map or **atlas** to plan your route.

2  Write down the details of your route and some of the things you will see on the way.

# Llandudno

Llandudno is in North Wales. It is situated on a **peninsula**, that juts out into the Irish Sea between two **headlands** called the Great Orme and the Little Orme.

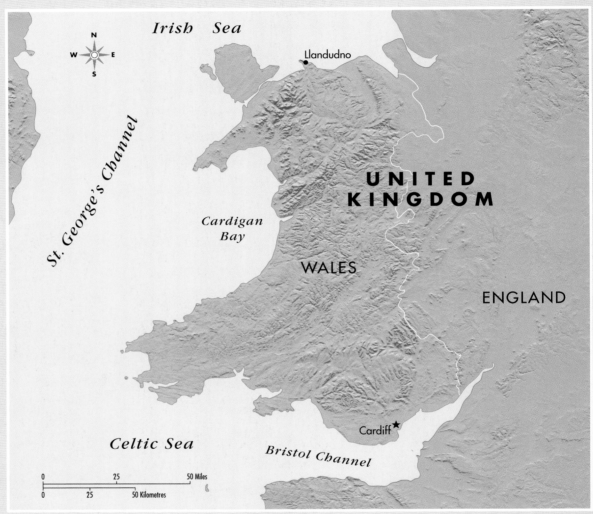

■ *This map of Wales shows the location of Llandudno.*

## What is Llandudno actually like?

Llandudno is a **coastal** resort town that is popular with holidaymakers, especially in the summer. There are lots of attractions for visitors, including the two main beaches. The busiest beach faces to the north and is backed by hotels built in Victorian times. This beach has a pier with amusements, cafes, and shops. The second, much quieter, beach faces west towards the island of Anglesey and is backed by sand **dunes**.

■ *One reason people come to visit Llandudno on their holidays is to relax on the long, sandy beaches.*

Many people choose to visit the Great Orme Country Park which is next to the town. The **summit** of the Great Orme can be reached by travelling on a tram or by taking a cable car. People go to the summit to see the great views of the town and out to sea. People also enjoy visiting some 4000-year-old copper mines and a ski and snowboard centre at the Great Orme.

## Activity

Look back at your list of all the things you could do on a weekend trip to Llandudno.

1  Now you know more about the place, write a detailed itinerary (day by day record of what you will do) for your weekend in Llandudno.
2  Say how long you would spend in each place or doing each activity, and how you would get around.

# What are the main similarities and differences between our local area and another area?

In geography we need to be able to compare our own area, or **locality**, with other areas. To do this, we need to be able to identify and understand the similarities and differences between them, and to explain why they occur. We can also think about the effects they have on the people living in each place.

### How to study the areas
We can study our own area directly by exploring it ourselves. As we have already seen, we can study another locality in two ways: by using **secondary sources,** such as encyclopedias and the Internet, or by doing fieldwork.

### Making comparisons
Once you have collected your secondary sources or done your fieldwork, think carefully about your findings and compare them with your own area. Make a note of any similarities or differences and try to explain the reasons for them. You can also look at the effect the **landscape** has on the people who inhabit it. Have your first thoughts about the place changed now that you have studied the location in detail?

## Activity

Compare your local area with Edinburgh or Llandudno.

1  What are the similarities and differences?

2  Can you explain the reasons for these?

The pictures on the opposite page might help you to draw up your list.

■ This is The Great Orme, Llandudno.

■ Edinburgh city centre.

## *Exploring further*

Read the articles on the cities of Bangalore, India and New York, USA on the Heinemann Explore website or CD-ROM to find out more about some contrasting localities. Go to Exploring > The World to find the articles. Look at the photographs that go with each article and compare these localities. Think about the land use, the **economic** activities, and the buildings in each location.

# Why is our locality the way it is?

By studying the geography of our **locality** we can find out not only what it is like, but also why it is like that. We can learn how people affect our **environment**. These are its human features. We can also look at how the physical features of our locality affect it and what we can do in it.

## Using maps

Maps can help us to find out more about why our locality is the way it is. From maps we can learn how high the land is above sea level, and whether it is flat or hilly. We can locate woodlands, farmland, rivers, and **quarries**. All these things will influence the types of **settlement** in the locality and what people living there do for work and leisure activities.

© Crown Copyright

■ *This OS map shows us that the area around Llandudno is **coastal** and hilly. We can tell the area is hilly because there are contour lines on the map. The closer together these lines are, the more hilly the area. You can tell that the area is coastal by the blue on the map, which represents the sea.*

## How the landscape can affect our locality

The **landscape** can affect our locality in many ways. It will affect the jobs we do and where we live. If people live near the coast, for example in Llandudno, they might be involved in the summer **tourist** industry, perhaps working in hotels. If they live in a **rural** area they might work in farming. What goes on in your local area that gives a lot of people jobs? Do they have to travel far to their work? Think about how the landscape affects your locality.

- *The coastal landscape around Llandudno influences what jobs people do and how they spend their leisure time.*

## Activity

Look at a map of your local area.

- Is it flat land or hilly land? How could this affect where people live?
- Is it in an area of farmland? If so, how could this affect the jobs people do?
- Are there any rivers nearby? If your locality is on a river that floods, how might this affect the buildings and the people living in the area?
- Are there any quarries nearby? If there are, what does this suggest about the type of work there is or might have been in the past?
- Are there many factories nearby? Looking at old maps can give clues about work during the past in towns.

# How the weather can affect our locality

The **weather** can also have an effect on our locality. In countries like the UK, where the weather can be very cold, some people have **double glazing** in their windows to keep the heat in. In warmer places, the walls of buildings are usually thinner than those in colder areas and they do not have **insulation**. In countries where there is a lot of rain, houses have pointed roofs so that the water can run off. In hot, sunny countries the roofs are often flat.

- *In a country like the UK, some homes have double glazing to help keep the heat inside.*

## Activity

Look at the walls and windows of buildings in your area.

1 What are they made of?

2 Do you notice any features that might be there because of our cold winter weather?

3 Does your house have double glazing? What does this do to your house? How does it affect you?

4 What other things might people do to their houses because of the weather?

## How history has affected our locality

Have you ever noticed anything historic in your area? Perhaps you live in a place where someone famous was born or lived, like William Shakespeare, Charles Dickens, or Winston Churchill, for example. Places like these attract tourists and have shops that sell all kinds of **souvenirs**. Maybe you live near an old castle, ruin, or fort, which attracts visitors. Perhaps your area was affected by the Second World War (1939–1945). Damage from bombs might have caused the area to be rebuilt after 1945.

■ *Edinburgh Castle was built to protect the city in* AD *600 on a huge volcanic rock called Castle Rock. For centuries it was the residence of the kings and queens of Scotland.*

## See for yourself

Take a walk around your local area.

- Is there anything historic in your area?
- Did anyone famous live there?
- Is there a castle, ruin, or fort?
- Was your area bombed during the Second World War?
- How have these factors affected your local area?

# What links do I have with other places in the world?

Did you know that you and your **locality** have connections with other places in the world? These connections or links exist in many different ways, such as through our families, holidays, television, food, and clothes.

## Family

You might be connected to other places by your family. Do any of your relatives live in different parts of the UK? Do you have any relatives in other countries around the world? If your relatives live in other countries, try to find those countries on a map of the world. If they live in the UK, try to locate their towns or cities on a map of the UK.

## Holidays

Holidays also connect us to the rest of the world. Think about the places you have been to on holiday.

- *These British children are on holiday in Egypt, North Africa.*

## Activity

1 Find the places you have been to on holiday in an atlas.

2 Do you have any postcards or photographs of where you went? Make a display about the places you have visited.

3 Describe the place you went to on holiday most recently. Or think of a place you would like to visit. Why do you want to go there?

4 What is the best way to get to this place, drive, fly, or go by boat. How long does the journey take?

## Television

Many television programmes and films come from the USA and Australia, and we see news stories from all over the world. Can you think of any countries that are in the news at the moment? Collect some newspaper cuttings of stories from around the world, then find these countries in an **atlas**.

## Food

Our food comes from many different countries. Look at some of the food packages in your fridge or cupboard. Try to identify where the food comes from. Here are some examples. Find these countries on a map of the world:

* tomatoes: Spain
* olives: Cyprus
* chocolate: Switzerland
* Edam cheese: The Netherlands

## Clothes

Many of your clothes were made in other countries of the world. Look at the labels inside them to find out where they were made. Find these countries on a map of the world.

■ *These olives growing in Cyprus will be eaten in the UK.*

# Looking at far away localities

## Cairo

Cairo is in the north of Egypt. It is the country's largest city, and its **capital** city. Cairo is on the River Nile, with the Nile **Delta** to the north, and **desert** to the east, west, and south. The city of Cairo can be reached in a number of ways and has an airport, a railway station, and a bus station.

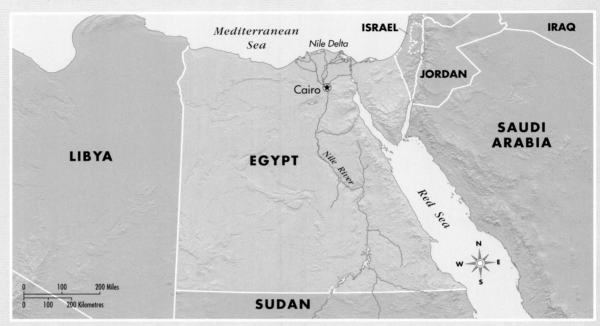

■ *This map shows the location of Cairo.*

## What is Cairo like?

Cairo has a **population** of 16.5 million people. It is an ancient city – people have been living there for more than 6000 years.

On the east bank of the Nile is Cairo's centre. This has a large, open square that is usually full of **tourists**. There are several attractions around the square, including the Egyptian Museum and the modern Umar **Mosque**. From north to south on the east bank of the River Nile runs Al Kurnish, Cairo's main road. There are a number of islands on the River Nile, these are linked to the city by bridges.

Outside the city's central area, on the east bank of the river, are the neighbourhoods of Islamic Cairo. These are known for their narrow streets, crowded **bazaars,** and hundreds of mosques, many dating back to **medieval** times. South of this is Old Cairo, where some of the city's oldest monuments are found. Modern **suburbs** have built up on the outskirts of the city in recent years.

■ *The most famous sights associated with Cairo are the ancient Egyptian pyramids and the Sphinx, which are located just outside the city. Both were built thousands of years ago.*

## Activity

1 Draw a map of Egypt. Label the three countries that border Egypt.

2 Mark these geographical features on your map: Suez Canal, Red Sea, Lake Nasser, River Nile, Sahara Desert.

3 Now mark on these cities: Suez, Aswan, Cairo, Port Said, Alexandria.

4 Colour your map to show the fertile and the dry areas of land. Remember to include a **key**.

5 What do you think it would be like to live in Egypt?

# Rhodes

The Greek islands are dotted all over the Ionian, Aegean, and Mediterranean Seas. There are over 1500 islands altogether, but only about 150 have people living on them. Crete is the largest island. It is in the Mediterranean Sea. The island of Rhodes is also in the Mediterranean Sea, and is shaped like a diamond. Rhodes is closer to Turkey than it is to mainland Greece.

■ This map shows the location of Rhodes.

## What is Rhodes like?

Rhodes is the fourth-largest Greek island. It has over 45 towns and villages and is, officially, the sunniest place in Europe. In winter it is mild, with lots of rain. In summer it is hot and sunny. It has warm waters to swim in and beaches that are mostly sandy.

Rhodes is a **mountainous** island, with thickly forested areas and many olive trees. It is a **tourist** resort, so at the **coast** there are plenty of water sports centres and many restaurants.

The capital of Rhodes is called Rhodes Town. This is an ancient, **medieval** town steeped in history. In some parts very little has changed for hundreds of years. Rhodes Town is at the island's most northerly point, and is bordered by the sea to the east and west.

■ *Rhodes is famous as an island of sun, sea, and sand.*

## Activity

1 Choose one of these Greek islands and put together an information leaflet about it: Corfu, Crete, Kos.

2 Draw a map of your island. Label the seas and the countries near it. Use an **atlas** to help you.

3 Using the Internet, textbooks, holiday brochures, and an atlas, find out about the island. In your research make sure you answer these questions:

- Where is your island?
- How will you get there?
- What will the **weather** be like?
- What does it look like?
- What types of plants and animals will you see there?
- How many people live there?

## Glossary

**aerial photograph**   picture taken from the air

**atlas**   book of maps

**bazaar**   outdoor market or shop

**capital city**   a country's most important city. It is usually where the government is based.

**coast**   land next to the sea

**delta**   fan-shaped area at the mouth of a river. It is made up of solid material that is left by the river as it enters the sea.

**desert**   large area of very dry, often sandy, land

**double glazing**   windows with two layers of glass to keep heat in or noise out

**dunes**   mounds of loose sand shaped by the wind

**environment**   natural and man-made things that make up our surroundings

**field trip**   visit to find out about a place by being there

**headland**   area of land that juts out into the sea

**human features**   all the things in a place made by humans, such as housing, factories, and roads

**insulation**   material put around the walls of a room, or a pipe, or in a roof to keep the heat inside

**key**   panel to explain the features on a map or graph

**landscape**   scenery and its features

**limestone**   type of rock

**locality**   the area around a place

**medieval**   from the period of history known as the Middle Ages

**mosque**   building where Muslims worship

**mountainous**   land with many mountains

**peninsula**   area of land that has water on three sides

**physical features**   natural features of a place, such as rivers, hills, and woodlands

**population**   the number of people living in a place

**port**   place on the coast or on a large river where ships load and unload their cargo

**quarry** a place where stone or slate is dug out of the ground

**rural**   in the countryside

**satellite photograph**   picture taken from a satellite in space

**secondary sources**   reference books, such as encyclopedias and the Internet

**settlement**   place where people live

**souvenir**   something to remind you of a place

**suburb**   built-up area on the outside edge of a town or city

**summit**   the top of a hill or mountain

**tourist**   person who visits a place for pleasure

**weather**   rain, snow, sunshine, cloud and wind at a particular time or place

## Find out more

### Books

*Philip's Junior School Atlas (4th edn)*, (Heinemann, Rigby, Ginn, 2003)

*Step up geography: Contrasting localities*, Ruth Nason and Julia Roche (Evans Brothers, 2005)

### Websites

*www.multimap.co.uk, or http://maps.google.co.uk*

By entering place names or postcodes, you can see aerial and satellite photographs, as well as maps of particular places and at different scales.

*www.ordnancesurvey.co.uk/mapzone*

You can play games, get homework help, and learn more about using Ordnance Survey maps on this website.

*www.heinemannexplore.com*

Discover more about different localities around the world on the Heinemann Explore website. Watch videos, use interactive maps, and see hundreds of photographs.

# Index

# Titles in the *Explore Geography* series include:

Hardback     0 431 03293 9

Hardback     0 431 03254 8

Hardback     0 431 03257 2

Hardback     0 431 03252 1

Hardback     0 431 03251 3

Hardback     0 431 03253 X

Hardback     0 431 03256 4

Hardback     0 431 03255 6

Find out about other titles from Heinemann Library on our website www.heinemann.co.uk/library